A driver greeted them in a traditional Hyderabadi style.

For Mom's meeting, they went to Hitech City. Shivi looked out of the window. The neat and clean roads, modern buildings and the smartly dressed people impressed Shivi.

Shivi behaved like a good boy and waited patiently. He did not disturb anybody while Mom was busy with her meeting.

Yes Mom, but I had finished my homework and was getting bored!

Mummy's meeting went well. She took Shivi for a special treat—Hyderabadi Biryani!

Shivi loved the aromatic smell of the Biryani at the restaurant. He loved the spicy taste too.

They went to India's first IKEA. Shivi loved to see furniture that he could make himself!

IKEA
Will I become a carpenter if I make a table myself?
What do you want to be when you grow up?

The next day, they had a fun outing. They were going to see the famous Golconda Fort. Shivi loved soldiers and he hoped he would meet some.

Fun Fact: Both the Kohinoor and Hope Diamonds are from Golconda.

He saw a hall where the sound could echo to a kilometer.
This clap was used to warn the kings in case of an attack.

Inside the fort is a huge Baobab tree which has a cavity so big that 40 people can fit inside. This tree is 600 years old.
In a town in Africa, there is a church built inside one of these trees!

Next day at the famous Charminar, Shivi was surprised by how different it was compared to the modern Hitech City.

In Hyderabadi language,
Kya hona= What do you want?
Hau= Yes Nakko= No
Kaiku= Why?

In the Laad Bazaar, outside Charminar, people were selling pearls, Bidriware, Kalamkari and lac bangles. Shivi was thrilled to hear the Hyderabadi language— it was so "mast"!

In the evening, when the sun was setting, they took a speedboat in Hussein Sagar near Lumbini Park where he saw the Big Buddha Statue and India's largest flag.

That flag is as big as three buses!

They went to the Dialogue in the Dark for Dinner. It was so dark inside that they could not see anything. The waiters were blind but they still did everything so easily.

But Shivi had a really difficult time. He had to use his other senses of smell, taste and touch instead of his eyes to understand what he was eating.

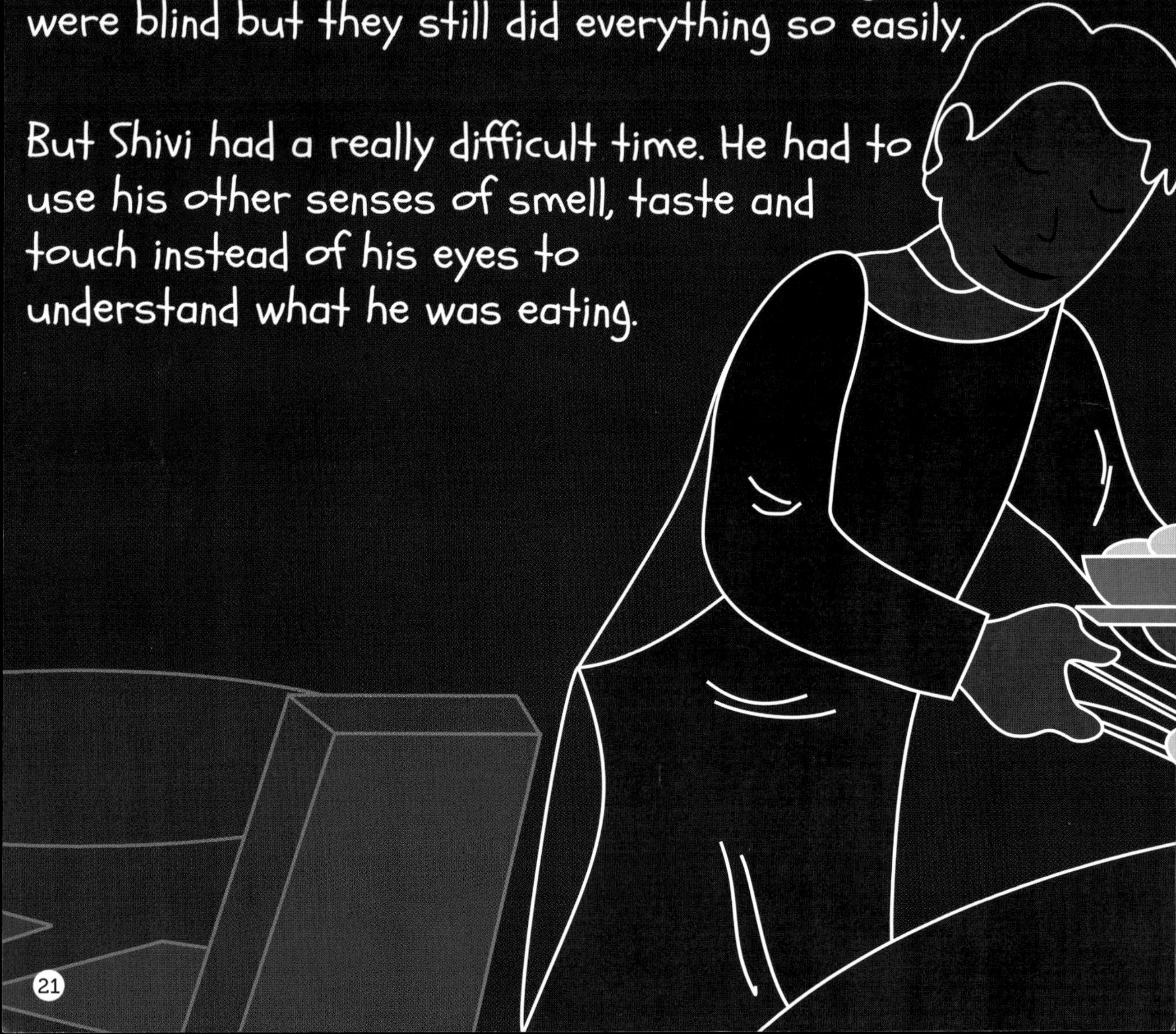

He was amazed at how the waiters were so good at their job. He learnt that even if people can't see, they can still do so much.

DiALOGUE iN THE DAR

Shivi was tired. He could not keep his eyes open. He knew he would fall if he walked with his eyes closed. He had eaten in the dark and now knew how difficult it was. He realised how lucky he was for his ability to see. He promised himself he would not spoil his eyes by spending too much time on the phone or iPad. And with that promise they returned home from Hyderabad.

Note For Parents:
Blindfold your child for some time depending on his age and ask him to do his regular chores. It will make them appreciate the gift of vision.

What do you enjoy most on your trips?

Date: